Avalanche and Landslide Alert!

Amanda Bishop & Vanessa Walker

Crabtree Publishing Company
www.crabtreebooks.com

presented by:

Crabtree Publishing Company

www.crabtreebooks.com

Coordinating editor: Ellen Rodger

Book design: Samara Parent, Rosie Gowsell

Cover design: Rob MacGregor

Production coordinator: Rosie Gowsell

Photo research: Allison Napier

Scanning Technician: Arlene Arch-Wilson

Consultant: Dr. Richard Cheel, Professor of Earth Sciences, Brock University

Photographs: AP Wide World Photos: p. 3, p. 4, p. 7 (bottom), p. 20, p. 25 (top) p. 26, p. 29 (all); James Balog: p.1; Betteman/Corbis: p.17 (top); Lloyd Cluff/Corbis: p. 18; Dennie Cody/Taxi/Getty Images: p. 9 (bottom); Per Erikkson/Getty Images: p. 21 (top); FEMA: p. 27 (bottom); Lowell Georgia/Corbis: p. 23; Larry Dale Gordon/Getty Images: p. 12 (bottom); Randall Hyman: p. 15; Jacques Janquox/Stone/Getty Images: p. 6; Heath A. Korvola/Liquid Light: p. 22 (top); Jacque Langevin/Corbis Sygma: p. 19; Mathis/Corbis Sygma: p. 28; Timothy O'Keefe/Index Stock Imagery: p. 27 (top); Panoramic Images/Getty Images: pp. 16-17 (bottom); Pic Impact/Corbis: p. 14; Ken Reid/Taxi/Getty Images: p.22 (bottom); David Samuel Robbins/Corbis & Magma: p. 5; Ivan Sekretarev: p. 7 (top); Qilai

Shen: p. 12 (top); Carl Tremblay/Index Stock Imagery: p. 8; Gordon Wiltsie/National Geographic Images Collection: p. 21 (bottom); Bob Winsett/Index Stock Imagery: p. 24

Illustrations: Dan Pressman: pp. 10-11, p.13; David Wysotski: pp. 30-31.

Cover: Vehicles lie buried in debris from a mudslide. The slide happened when severe rains washed away a hillside and sent mud and rocks hurtling downhill.

Contents: A mudslide and rockslide caused by wet weather carried away homes and stepped farming fields on a mountainside.

Title page: Cars and vans lie tossed and crumpled after a powerful avalanche buried a mountain highway. People who live near mountains are aware of the constant danger of avalanches in winter and spring and rockslides in summer and fall.

Crabtree Publishing Company

www.crabtreebooks.com   1-800-387-7650

Cataloging-in-Publication data

Bishop, Amanda.
    Avalanche and landslide alert! / written by Amanda Bishop and Vanessa Walker.
        p. cm. -- (Disaster alert!)
    Includes index.
    ISBN 0-7787-1576-0 (rlb) -- ISBN 0-7787-1608-2 (pbk)
    1. Avalanches--Juvenile literature. 2. Landslides--Juvenile literature.
I. Walker, Vanessa, 1971- II. Title. III. Series.
    QC929.A8B48 2005
    551.3'07--dc22

2004013052
LC

**Published in
the United States**
PMB 16A
350 Fifth Ave.,
Suite 3308
New York, NY
10118

**Published
in Canada**
616 Welland Ave.,
St. Catharines,
Ontario, Canada
L2M 5V6

**Published in the
United Kingdom**
73 Lime Walk,
Headington,
Oxford
0X3 7AD
United Kingdom

**Published
in Australia**
386 Mt. Alexander Rd.,
Ascot Vale (Melbourne)
V1C 3032

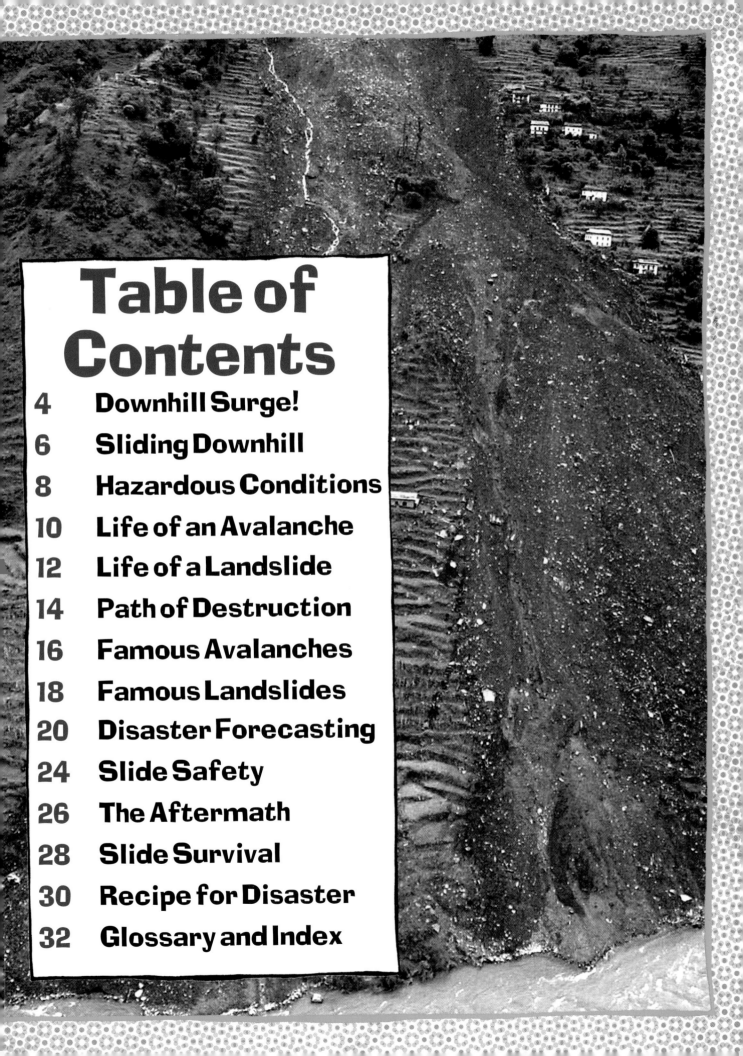

Table of Contents

Downhill Surge!

Mountainous or hilly areas of the world are prone to three kinds of slides. Avalanches are masses of snow that surge down mountains, snapping trees and tossing giant boulders. Land and rockslides are huge amounts of rock and soil that move down slopes, carrying away anything in their path.

The power of an avalanche, landslide, or rockslide can be overwhelming. Trees, buildings, and living things that lie in their paths are swept away. They can cause enormous amounts of damage and smother victims under heavy snow or mud.

A helicopter views the scene of an avalanche. Towering blocks of snow mark where the avalanche barrelled down a mountainside.

What is a disaster?
A disaster is a destructive event that affects the natural world and human communities. Some disasters are predictable and others occur without warning. Coping successfully with a disaster depends on a community's preparation.

Looking and learning

For people who live in valleys and on mountainsides, avalanches and rockslides are real and **persistent** threats. People used to think these powerful slides were acts of nature that could not be avoided. Today, scientists and people who live on mountains know about the conditions in which avalanches and landslides take place.

Geologists and **meteorologists** are the scientists who study these disasters to understand their causes. They study why slides occur, when they are most likely to happen, and how best to avoid them. Scientists can even make avalanche or landslide predictions and warn people who might be in danger.

Mountain Spirits

People who live in mountainous parts of the world often believe that their mountains are special, magical places where gods or spirits live. Some people believe that angered gods or spirits cause deadly avalanches and landslides. People honor their mountain spirits by marking rocks and hanging flags and prayer wheels, hoping to prevent mountain disasters. In some mountain communities, avalanches were commonly called the White Dragon or the White Death. Children in the Alps mountains of Europe learned folk stories about the avalanche beast, who could fly without wings, strike without hands, and see without eyes. Some people have blamed witches for causing avalanches and landslides. The Tibetan people who live near the Himalaya mountain range in central Asia still fly pieces of cloth at the base of the mountains to honor the mountain spirits.

In the Himalayas, the world's largest mountain range, Tibetan sherpas, or mountain guides and porters, hang flags and pieces of cloth at the base of the mountain to please the mountain spirits. The sherpas make their living by helping people climb the mountains.

Sliding Downhill

Avalanches and landslides are both examples of mass wasting. Mass wasting happens when gravity forces heaps of earth, debris, or snow down a mountain or hill slope. Avalanches and landslides may be triggered by many different events, such as heavy rain or snow, and earthquakes.

Slopes and sliding

All mountains, hills, or cliffs have slopes, or inclines. Slopes are either steep or gentle, depending on the degree of angle, or grade. The steeper a slope is, the larger its angle. A slope with an angle of 50 percent is considered steep. Loose rock, soil, or snow is less likely to slide when it rests on a slope with an angle of 35 degrees or less.

Stability

Snow and soil naturally build up on slopes. Under certain conditions, such as heavy rain, their weight changes and makes them less stable. Once unstable, soil, rocks, and snow can slide down the slope in a great mass.

The grab of gravity

Gravity is the force that pulls all objects toward the Earth. Gravity acts on material that is built up on a slope in two ways. Gravity pulls the material against the slope's surface, as well as down to the bottom of the slope. In normal conditions, these two pulls are balanced, and soil, rock, or snow stays put. The angle where soil or snow is most likely to remain stable, is called the angle of repose.

Soil, rock, and even vegetation slide off this hillside in Guatemala because the soil has been eroded, or wasted away, through overfarming and heavy rains.

A valley in Russia shows a worn avalanche path and a glacier. People who live in valleys must be aware of the potential for avalanches in winter and rockslides in summer.

Structure

Materials such as snow, rock, and **regolith** often collect to form piles, or masses. A collection of snowflakes creates a mass called a snow pack. When a mass sticks together well, it is called cohesive. Friction, or the rubbing action between rocks, stones, or snow makes a mass more cohesive, or able to stick together. Heavy rain or snow makes the rocks, stones, or snow less cohesive. When rain falls on a snow pack, for instance, smooth water droplets slide between the snowflakes, lessening the friction between them. This makes the snow less likely to cling to a slope, and more likely to fall in an avalanche.

The force of an avalanche from heavy snow cleared a path down a steep mountainside in Chamonix, France.

Hazardous Conditions

Wind, snow, rain, and temperature can make the difference between a stable snow pack and an avalanche. Sometimes, avalanches are set off, or triggered, by skiers on hill slopes.

Wind and avalanches

Under normal conditions, snow accumulates on mountainsides slowly, at an average rate of one foot (0.3 meters) per hour. When wind blows during a snowfall, it carries the snow at greater speeds and also picks up fallen snow from the ground. Some mountain slopes can have much more snow on them than has actually fallen. On mountains, the wind blows across a mountain's windward side, or the side that faces the wind. The wind carries snow to the peak's leeward side, or the side that is sheltered from the wind. The leeward side rapidly collects large amounts of snow, creating the perfect conditions for an avalanche.

Watch out!

The added weight of a heavy snowfall upsets the balance of gravity by making a snow pack unstable. An unstable snow pack can be dislodged as an avalanche by something as simple as wind, or a skier. Land and rockslides happen when rain or wind force rock, soil, or debris down a slope. The moving rock gains speed and additional debris as it slides down the hill slope.

A cornice is a mass of snow or ice formed by the wind that overhangs the rocky slope. Any pressure added to the cornice of snow could collapse the entire structure. Some mountains have posted avalanche warnings for skiers.

Skiing on fresh, unstable snow can trigger avalanches.

Sunlight and temperature

Sunlight and temperature also have an impact on avalanches. When a layer of snow on a mountainside is warmed by the sun during the day, it begins to melt. When night falls and the temperature drops, the layer of snow refreezes into crystals. If a heavy snowfall follows the refreezing, the weak layer of refrozen snow, or **hoar crystals**, is buried under the new snow. As fresh snow accumulates, the snow pack becomes heavier. Hoar crystals make the snow pack unstable because they do not stick to other types of snow. The snow may appear packed and safe, but the weak layer below is an avalanche waiting to happen.

Setting it off

A number of conditions create the perfect circumstances for an avalanche or a landslide, but all that is needed is a single event to set off a disaster. Landslides are often triggered by other natural disasters, such as very heavy rainfall, earthquakes, or volcanic eruptions. These events upset the stability of the rock and a fracture, or break, occurs in the mass, sending it down the mountainside. Avalanches are usually triggered by vibrations that disturb a weak layer under the snow pack.

A landslide washed away a hillside and highway in Washington state.

Life of an Avalanche

There are several types of avalanches, each caused by different conditions. Avalanches range in size from small amounts of snow kicked up by skiers to deadly masses of snow that slide with enough force to level villages.

Dry or wet

Avalanche experts usually divide avalanche types into two categories: wet and dry. Wet avalanches occur when the snow is saturated, or heavy with water. Saturation happens when surface layers of snow melt and drip down into lower layers, making the snow pack slick and unstable. Glide avalanches and slush avalanches are two other types of wet avalanches.

Wet avalanches commonly occur in spring or during midwinter thaws. Glide avalanches happen when a small layer of water builds between the slope surface and the bottom layer of snow and sends it downhill. Slush avalanches are most common on gentle slopes. They begin when melting snow adds weight and sends the mass of slush downhill.

Unstable snow pack slides down a mountainside

The avalanche topples trees as it hurtles downhill.

Wind

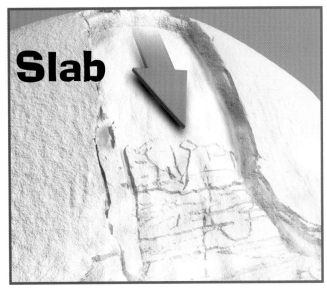

Slab

Powder fall

Dry avalanches are caused by factors other than added water weight. Dry avalanches include slab avalanches, loose or powder avalanches, cornice falls, and ice avalanches. Loose avalanches happen when a surface layer of snow is disturbed, causing clouds of snow to rush down the mountainside, fanning out into a triangle as it moves. Cornice falls happen when wind causes the snow to drift and accumulate in layers. The weight of the snow, or wind, eventually sends the snow hurtling down.

Slab fall

Slab avalanches often threaten skiers. A slab avalanche occurs when an area of compressed, or hard-packed, snow separates from surrounding snow and flies down the mountain as a giant mass. Wet slab avalanches happen when snow thaws or mixes with rain and the snowpack loosens and slides down the hill. Ice avalanches are caused when a chunk of ice breaks away near the top of a mountain **crag** and starts rolling. The ice accumulates rock and snow as it travels downhill.

Hurling rocks

Summer and fall are rockslide seasons in mountainous regions. After winter snow melts and frost leaves the soil, rocks expand and are often dislodged from mountain slopes. Spring rains moisten the soil and add weight to precarious rock. Mountain roads can be dangerous places in slide season. Rocks can crush car roofs.

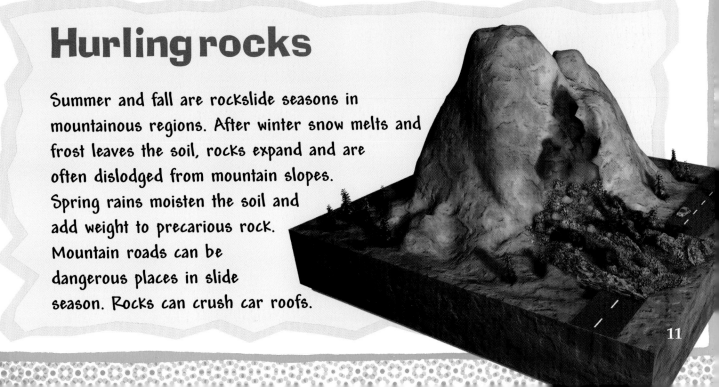

Life of a Landslide

Land and rockslides often happen after severe rains or earthquakes. The mud, rock, and debris of a landslide are heavy, fast-moving, and very difficult to escape.

Types of landslides

Landslides are frightening and powerful flows of earth. Geologists divide landslides into two categories: slope failures and sediment flow. Slope failures include slides, falls, and slumps. A slope "fails" when weight causes part of the slope to break away from a hill, sending debris downhill. Sediment, or slurry flows, may be wet or dry.

Failing grades

Flows occur when debris is carried downhill, usually because of **precipitation** or wind. Slides, falls, and slumps are called slope failures because they change the structure of the slope, hill, or mountainside.

Slides are similar to slab avalanches because large slabs of land break away from the slope's surface and slide downward. Falls occur when large chunks of rock or regolith break away from the slope and crash downward. In hilly areas where falls are common, piles of talus, or debris, are found directly below a steep cliff.

(above) **A mule handler helps his animal over a rockslide on the Karakorum highway in Pakistan.**

Anchors such as trees and boulders can interrupt the flow of a landslide. In places where trees have been cut down or have burned in fires, the danger of landslides may increase. Water can flow more quickly over slopes without anchors, picking up debris as it moves.

Landslide

When a landslide happens, land breaks away from high ground. When the rock breaks away, it sometimes forms a scarp, a mound that looks like a cliff.

The weight of wet soil, gravel, sand, and other debris forces a hill slope to "slump" and break away from a hill. Debris deposits at the toe, or bottom, of the slide.

Creep is the very slow movement of soil over time. As the soil slowly settles, expands, and contracts, objects such as signposts, telephone poles, and gravestones start to tilt over time. Soil is always creeping, so the phenomenon can be difficult to observe.

Going with the flow

Sediment flows are caused by pressure, usually from air or water, that causes debris to move over a slope like water. Dry or granular flows have little water, while wet or slurry flows are at least twenty percent water. Granular flows such as grain flows and debris avalanches carry particles mixed with air downhill, often at great speeds. Slurry flows such as mudflows and debris flows carry volumes of wet debris and regolith. A lahar is a volcanic mudflow, often caused by a volcanic eruption, that occurs when a wet flow mixes with volcanic ash as it travels down the side of a volcano.

Path of Destruction

Once an avalanche or landslide has been triggered, there is no stopping the slide. Many avalanches and landslides take place high in the mountains, far from human observers. Slides are disasterous when they strike a mountain community, skiers or climbers, or towns located at the toe.

In harm's way

Long ago, people were wary of mountains and avoided venturing onto them unless it was absolutely necessary. Today, millions of people live on mountainsides around the world, always aware that they are living in harm's way. Mountain areas are prone to rockslides during the summer and fall. In the winter and early spring, avalanches are a threat. People who live on mountains or in valleys know that rockslides and avalanches can block highways and make life difficult. As more people move to these areas, the natural anchors, such as trees and ground cover, are stripped to make room for homes and ski resorts. When the anchors are gone, nothing stands between people and the slides that may start on the hills above them.

Some mountain, or alpine communities build snow fences on the sides of mountains. The fences help slow avalanches by blocking their paths.

The town of Isafjordu in Iceland is located at the bottom of a steep cliff and edge of an icy fjord. Townspeople are aware of the ever present rockslide and avalanche risk.

Forces unleashed

When an avalanche or landslide begins, everything in the path of the slide is in danger. Burial and destruction are two of the biggest risks. The rock, mud, snow, or ice of the slide can weigh thousands of tons, giving it more than enough material to cover roads, homes, and other buildings. Much of the damage to structures caused by giant slides is irreparable. Cars and buildings are smashed. Rocks are hurled and trees are uprooted and carried over distances. A landslide may also deposit in a river or a drainage ditch, damming it and causing flooding.

Massive attack

The tons of debris surging down a slope gather **momentum** as they move. By the time the slide reaches the lowest part of the track or **glide zone**, it is much more powerful than it was at the top. A large amount of debris accumulates in the toe, or turnout zone. Anything buried there may be covered by several feet of debris. The chances of survival for people who get buried are only as good as their air supply. Some people have survived burial for several hours because they had a pocket of air to breathe. Others have **suffocated** within minutes.

15

Famous Avalanches

Many of the world's biggest avalanches and landslides happen, luckily, in areas where people do not live: high up on mountains or in remote valleys. The most devastating avalanches and landslides hit communities where people live. They swallow homes, destroy property, and kill people.

Hannibal and the mountains

One of the most famous avalanches in history occurred over 2,000 years ago. In 218 B.C., in the European Alps, legendary warrior and leader Hannibal attempted to guide his army of 38,000 men, 8,000 horses, and 37 elephants across the mountains in heavy snow. As the animals and men crossed the mountainside, an avalanche began, killing 18,000 men, 2,000 horses, and many elephants.

The Himalayas, the mountain range in which Mount Everest is located, have more avalanches than any other place on Earth.

Everest, 1995

In November of 1995, several avalanches charged down Mount Everest, the world's tallest mountain in the Himalaya range of Central Asia. On November 11, an avalanche swallowed an entire hiking group in Nepal. By the time rescuers arrived at the group's campsite, 26 people had been killed. The next day, 59 climbers, guides, and local residents died in another avalanche. Nepalese helicopter pilots braved wind and blinding snow to airlift over 200 people off the mountain to safety.

Getting the goat

In the late 1700s, a book was written to record the incredible story of three women in Italy who survived an avalanche. The women were trapped in a stable when an avalanche roared down the mountain, but the building did not collapse. Instead, the women were able to survive for 37 days in the air pocket created in the stable. They drank the milk of a goat and, according to legend, even delivered a baby goat while waiting to be rescued!

Peru, 1962

The second-tallest mountain in South America, North Huascaran, was the site of a devastating rock and mudslide avalanche on January 10, 1962. A piece of ice approximately 3 million cubic yards (1,780 cubic meters) broke off the mountain's **ice cap** and fell onto a glacier below, triggering an avalanche that eventually contained as much as 13 million cubic yards (7,713 cubic meters) of ice, snow, soil, and regolith. At least 4,000 people were killed in this **catastrophe**.

Alaska, 1981

An avalanche on Mount Sandford in Alaska traveled eight miles (13 km) before stopping. On its journey, the avalanche moved from an elevation of 10,000 feet (3,048 meters), then careened up and over a 3,000 foot (914 meters) mountain and down the other side. A powder cloud created by the avalanche was so tall that it could be seen from 100 miles (161 km) away.

(top right) A young girl sits in the rubble of her home in Ranrahirca, Peru. A landslide on Peru's largest mountain wiped out several villages below the mountain. (right) Milk from a goat kept three Italian women alive for 37 days after an avalanche swept over their mountain barn in the 1700s.

Famous Landslides

Landslides usually occur without warning. They bury houses, cars, crops, and people under a dirty mess of mud and rock. Some of the worst landslides happen because of earthquakes and volcanoes.

Landslide in Peru

In 1970, only eight years after a devastating avalanche in 1962, a strong earthquake rocked the North Huascaran mountain in the Peruvian Andes. The earthquake caused a terrible landslide with a debris flow that was about 3,000 feet (914 meters) wide and one mile (1.6 km) long. It took less than five minutes for the flow to reach the town of Yungay and completely bury it. The slide, at times traveling as fast as 250 miles (402 km) per hour, destroyed another village, and threw enormous boulders distances of 2,000 feet (610 meters). About 18,000 people were killed and thousands more were left homeless.

Years after a killer landslide roared through mountain villages below Peru's Mount Huascaran, debris such as this bus, still littered the area. The bus, buried in a permenant heap, shows the power of the landslide.

Lahar in Colombia

In 1985, a volcano called Nevado del Ruiz erupted in Colombia. The eruption caused ice at the top of the mountain to melt. The water carried mud and regolith down the slope, but the slides soon mixed with volcanic ash to form **lahars**. The giant flows killed more than 23,000 people.

Rockfall at Yosemite

On July 10, 1996, in Yosemite National Park in California, a massive rock weighing 32,000 tons (29,030 kg) separated from the canyon wall and fell toward the valley at an amazing 220 miles (354 km) per hour. The power of its fall was so great that it created fierce winds that knocked down 500 trees. One person was killed after being struck by a falling tree.

The Storegga landslides

Scientists believe that between 5,000 and 50,000 years ago, a series of landslides took place on the coast of Norway. One massive slope failure pushed rock and regolith into the ocean. The **displacement** of water created a series of **tidal waves** that traveled to the shores of Scotland and carried debris 311 miles (500 km) underwater.

Rescuers give water to a boy swept away by a volcano lahar in Colombia.

Disaster Forecasting

Predicting avalanches and landslides requires a lot of knowledge of the land. Scientists study where slides are most likely to take place and under what conditions. Research is important to keep people aware of the risks they may be taking when building a home or planning a trip into a danger zone.

Danger zone

Researchers keep detailed records of landslides and avalanches in order to know how they happen and whether they are likely to happen again in the same spot. Inventories are records that are put together in atlases or databases that make it easier for experts to track events and analyze geological trends.

Soil and rock cover a highway after a rockslide in the mountains of Switzerland.

Disaster forecasters

Meteorologists, or scientists who forecast the weather, work closely with avalanche and landslide experts to warn of weather that may create landslides or avalanches. One of the biggest risks is heavy precipitation. Slide experts also work closely with geologists studying earthquakes and volcanoes, since quakes and eruptions are often to blame for setting off large slides.

Many ski resorts deliberately set off controlled avalanches in the early hours of the morning. These small avalanches help restore the angle of repose on the slopes, getting rid of loose snow that could destabilize the snow pack when skiers are on slopes. Controlled avalanches are started by explosives.

Knowing the material

Scientists study the **grade** of slopes, the composition of different types of soil, and the effect of water on rock and regolith. Avalanche research began in the 1930s in Switzerland, a mountainous country with many villages in avalanche territory. Since then, avalanche research institutes have developed around the world. All are dedicated to the scientific study of snow. Their goal is to limit the number of dangerous avalanches. Sometimes, preventing dangerous avalanches involves setting off smaller, or "controlled" avalanches in mountain areas with heavy or unstable snow. Ski resorts set off explosives high in the mountains to rid slopes of loose snow.

Let it snow

The frozen ice crystals that form snowflakes have fascinated scientists for more than 400 years. Researchers at the International Commission on Snow and Ice divide snowflakes into ten different categories of basic shape. Snowflakes change their shape as they fall. Like ice, snowflakes are clear. Each flake refracts, or bends, light. The effect overwhelms the human eye with color, which is why people see snow as white, or a combination of all colors.

Collecting information

One of the keys to successful avalanche monitoring and warning systems is collecting accurate information. Scientists gather information with a wide variety of sensors, traps, and photographs. Mechanical devices are used to collect soil samples and measure snowfall. Sensors are used to detect sound vibrations, which indicates movement under the ground. Landscape changes are noted, and snow pack depth and stability are monitored. Aerial photographs and **radar** systems are used to determine areas of risk. Teams of avalanche experts monitor information gathered from data collection stations every hour and make reports on which mountain slopes are safe and which ones are dangerous. These reports are sent to ski hills, where skiers are warned of which slopes to stay away from.

A common language

Avalanche reports and landslide condition warnings are issued by scientists who monitor conditions in mountainous areas. Warnings are announced on radio, television, and sometimes on warning signs on the mountain itself. Others use systems of lights and sirens to alert people to emergencies. Some landslides and avalanches can affect places far from their origin, because the debris can travel far distances. For example, submarine landslides, which are slides that occur underwater, affect sea **currents** far from where the landslide occurred.

Landslide warning systems

On average, landslides kill about 1,000 people every year all over the world. Local warning systems allow scientists to issue specific warnings about slopes and weather conditions. Regional and national systems help establish records and coordinate emergency efforts. In Europe, some countries have chosen to use a common system of warnings so that travelers from foreign countries can understand which areas are safe and which are dangerous.

Levels of danger

Most avalanche warnings are color-coded and have five levels of danger. Green, or low hazard conditions mean there is little risk of avalanche. Yellow or moderate hazard warnings warn that some slopes have snow packs that are not stable. During an orange, or considerable hazard, warning the snow pack in many areas is unstable or even weak, and the danger is high for people who are inexperienced in avalanche conditions.

Red or high hazard conditions warn that the snow pack is weak enough to be triggered by almost anything. Very high or extreme hazard warnings, marked as red with a black border, mean that conditions are so bad that no one should be skiing in them.

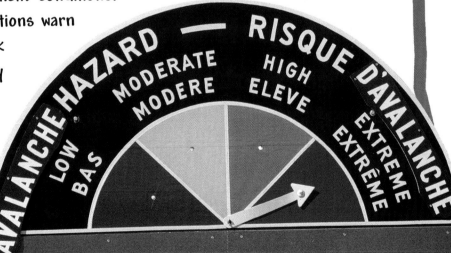

Slide Safety

Almost 90 percent of people endangered by avalanches were actually involved in triggering the avalanche. Avalanche and landslide safety begins with knowing the dangers, listening to the experts, and always being prepared for a disaster.

Know the mountains

Avalanches and landslides often recur in the same area. Avalanche routes are sections of mountains that have been cleared of trees and brush by previous avalanches. Many landslides leave a visible track on a slope that looks like a sand castle after water has been poured down one side. These tell-tale signs are clear warnings that a slope is prone to avalanches and landslides.

Avalanche safety

Avalanche experts warn skiers and tourists to avoid traveling across the leeward side of a mountain, even when their instincts tell them to get out of the wind. The leeward side of a mountain often has a buildup of unstable snow brought by wind. Staying safe on an avalanche-prone mountain means being aware of the dangers. Experts check snow pack stability by cutting into the snow and observing and testing the strength of snow layers with their hands or instruments. People who work on mountains sometimes use a beacon, an electronic device that sends out and receives **radio wave** signals. Before heading out for the day, they set their beacons to transmit so that if an avalanche happens, rescuers will be able to locate them. Rescuers set their beacons to receive, and they track the radio signals to find people who are buried under the snow.

Probes are collapsible metal wands that a rescuer pushes into the snow to feel for survivors. Rescuers also use dogs who can sniff out survivors, and tools such as lightweight shovels to dig people out. There is no sure way to survive an avalanche but people can lessen their risk.

Landslide safety

Governments monitor landslides in areas that have been identified as risky, but there is little equipment that can help individuals in a landslide. When weather conditions create a landslide alert, it is important for people in the region to keep a close eye on their surroundings, or evacuate the area. Sudden changes in the flow of nearby streams could indicate flooding or a landslide dam blocking the waterway. Sounds such as cracking or tumbling may indicate that trees or boulders are being dislodged by a slide or flow.

Watching the weather may be one of the only ways to prepare for a rock or landslide.

Set up a plan

Skiers and people who live in mountainous areas should always be aware of avalanche dangers and make plans for surviving a disaster. Plans should include:

- Evacuation plans or a safe place to go.
- A disaster relief kit that includes food, water, first-aid supplies, and medicines.
- The most important thing to remember during a storm that may trigger landslides is to stay awake. People who sleep through a landslide are much less likely to escape it.

Local governments often have emergency procedures and emergency response teams such as search and rescue teams. Some ski resorts also have employees with avalanche-risk training to keep an eye on conditions and be involved in rescue missions. Heed warning signs such as: deep cracking or groaning sounds or snow that collapses when it is stepped on. Carry safety gear, such as a shovel and a probe.

The Aftermath

Rescue efforts must begin immediately after an avalanche and landslide has stopped moving. In most cases, survivors are the most important rescuers. A climber may be able to locate his or her climbing partner who has been buried and start digging right away.

Avalanche rescue

The main risks to avalanche victims are suffocation, injuries such as broken bones, and **hypothermia**. People trapped by an avalanche are often unable to move once the avalanche stops because the snow sets like concrete. Buried victims have a good chance of survival if they are dug out within fifteen minutes. If survivors are unable to locate a companion buried in an avalanche, they should go for help, leaving markers so that the rescuers will be able to find their way back to the site.

Search and rescue

Emergency response teams organized by governments, aid agencies, local communities, and ski resorts are called to assist after an avalanche or landslide. Since time is limited, these rescue teams are called to duty quickly and on very short notice.

Visual clues, such as articles of clothing or athletic equipment, help rescuers to determine where they should start digging. Rescuers use long poles stuck in the snow to locate people.

Landslide recovery

In most serious landslides, victims are rarely recovered. Victims are usually crushed or suffocated by the rock and mud. Rescuers are left to clean up the debris and bury victims once they have been recovered. Search and rescue organizations, including government emergency workers and international aid organizations such as the **Red Cross/Red Crescent** help communities where landslides have occurred. After cleanup, the community must decide whether or not to rebuild in the area of the slide. People often choose not to build on the site again. Sites of great destruction are often left, sometimes because there is nobody left to rebuild or live there.

Often it is not safe to reenter a home half-destroyed by a landslide. Walls may collapse and injure people. Lives are never the same after a disaster such as a landslide or mudslide, even if people can rebuild their homes. They feel unsafe and mourn the loss of momentoes such as family photos.

Slide Survival

The people who are most likely to survive an avalanche or a landslide are those who are prepared. They have learned about the dangers in the area, have checked with the experts about the risks on a given day, prepared themselves with equipment or survival kits, and have practiced procedures such as probing the snow or evacuating their homes.

Knowing the basics

Experts in avalanche and landslide safety have many ideas about how best to survive a disaster. Many organizations offer avalanche courses that prepare winter athletes for the dangers of the mountains. Governments often publish reports on areas that are at risk for landslides in order to inform local residents of the risks. Warnings and suggestions are only useful if people pay attention to them.

A helicopter lands to airlift 35 people from a mountain after a massive avalanche in Austria. The survivors were located on the avalanche's fringes.

Do not gasp for air if caught in an avalanche. The snow moves with such force that it can block a person's airway in very little time. It may be safer to be buried in a building with sturdy walls and air pockets.

Avalanche survival guide

Avalanche experts say most avalanches happen so quickly that there is no time to remember what to do. Most agree that the most important thing a person should do is cover their face with their hands. This will help create a small pocket of air. Other tips for avalanche survival include:

1. Staying calm to conserve energy and air. It may be useful to yell for help, but snow creates a strong sound barrier.

2. Move in a swimming motion to avoid getting buried deep beneath the avalanche. This works best when caught near the top layers of the avalanche.

3. The backstroke is a victim's best bet for survival. Victims buried face-up survive much more frequently than those buried face-down.

Recipe For Disaster

Here is an easy experiment you can do to understand how mud and rockslides happen. Make sure you record your observations and clean up your mess!

What you need:

* two old, empty, one-inch 3-ring binders
* a pail of dirt from the backyard
* an old large aluminum-foil pan
* a pitcher with water
* four or five stones of different sizes
* a protractor
* a ruler
* a notebook in which to record your findings

What to do:

1. In the aluminum pan, lay one of the binders on its back. Use your protractor to measure the angle of the slope. Take a small handful of dirt and gently place it at the top of the slope. Measure the distance from the top of the slope to where the dirt stops sliding down the binder.

2. Brush the dirt off the surface before placing the second binder on top of the first binder. Measure the new angle with your protractor. Repeat step one, observing how far the dirt travels down the slope.

3. Pour a small amount of water onto the handful of dirt on the slope. Observe how the water carries the dirt along. Add more dirt to the slope, and try to pour water again. Observe the difference in the flow you have created.

4. Add more dirt to the slope. Then place a few pebbles at various points in the dirt. Try pouring the water again. How do the pebbles affect the flow of the landslide?

What you will see:

You have now created your own mudslide. Keep a record of all your observations in the notebook. You should find that the steeper the angle, the less stable the dirt. The water makes the dirt more likely to slide.

Glossary

catastrophic Describing a sudden disaster and its ruinous effects

conserve To keep from loss and for future use

crag A steep, rugged rock

currents Large bodies of air or water in motion

displacement The weight of liquid that is moved by something floating in it

evacuate To send people away from a dangerous place

fjord A long and narrow sea inlet located between steep cliffs

geologist A person who studies rocks and materials in the Earth's surface

glide zone An area whereby debris moves smoothly down a slope

grade The degree of a slope's incline

gravity The force that pulls objects toward the center of the Earth

hoar crystals Crystals of frozen dew that form a white coating on a surface

hypothermia Abnormally low body temperature

ice cap A dome-shaped covering of ice and snow that covers a large area of land

meteorologist A scientist who studies weather

momentum The force or speed of an object in motion

persistent Constantly repeated or lasting a long time

phenomenon An occurrence that can be observed

precipitation Moisture from the atmosphere deposited on the surface of the Earth

pressure A force exerted upon something

radar A system of detecting faraway objects using radio waves

radio waves Energy waves that carry signals between points without using wires

Red Cross/Red Crescent An international organization that cares for people sick, wounded, or homeless by wars or disaster

regolith The layer of loose rock located on top of bedrock

repose The state of being at rest

suffocated Killed by blocking access to air

tidal waves Large waves of water often caused by storms

Index

1 2 3 4 5 6 7 8 9 0   Printed in the U.S.A.   3 2 1 0 9 8 7 6 5 4